The Beginner's Guide to Embracing Femininity

By

Delphien Walker

Copyright © 2025 by Savannah Delphien Walker

All rights reserved. No part of this publication may be reproduced, distributed, or transmitted in any form or by any means, including photocopying, recording, or other electronic or mechanical methods, without the prior written permission of the publisher, except in the case of brief quotations embodied in critical reviews and certain other noncommercial uses permitted by copyright law.

Table Of Contents

DEDICATION 1

ACKNOWLEDGMENT 2

CHAPTER ONE UNDERSTANDING FEMININITY 4

CHAPTER TWO THE PHYSICAL EXPRESSION OF FEMININITY 6

CHAPTER THREE THE EMOTIONAL AND SPIRITUAL DIMENSIONS OF FEMININITY 10

CHAPTER FOUR INTEGRATING FEMININITY IN MODERN LIFE 13

CHAPTER FIVE SACRED PRACTICES - SIX GATEWAYS TO FEMININE ENERGY 16

    1. THE MORNING RITUAL - AWAKENING YOUR FEMININE FLOW 16

    2. THE SACRED PAUSE - CREATING MOMENTS OF PRESENCE 17

    3. THE SENSUAL FEAST - AWAKENING YOUR PHYSICAL WISDOM 17

    4. THE CIRCLE OF SISTERS - CULTIVATING FEMININE CONNECTION ... 18

    5. THE EMBODIED DANCE - MOVING WITH YOUR FEMININE POWER ... 18

    6. THE EVENING SURRENDER - HONORING YOUR CYCLICAL NATURE 19

Dedication

To all the readers ready for a sacred foundation to return to when feeling further from their true feminine selves.

Acknowledgment

With special appreciation to these incredible teachers along my journey; I thank my mother, Tina-teaching me sacred dance stabilizes moods. Respect and kindness are available to all those we meet, a concept I learned by example from Erica, Monica and Jessica, my eldest cousins. The art of bold honesty my sister Mackenzie graced me with. I share my appreciation to Ella Harrison for showcasing authentic spirituality, and Cynthia Loewen for her wonderful work in the feminine development to those ready to learn, and a special thanks to Adrienne Everheart for coaching how to feel emotions rather than denying them- and to Mother Moon for illuminating my spirit. And Diane Dreher for saving it with *The Tao of Inner Peace*.

Chapter One
Understanding Femininity

Imagine standing before an ancient mirror, catching glimpses not just of your reflection, but of countless women across time and culture who have explored the same question: What does it mean to be feminine?

Femininity, in its most fundamental form, represents a complex tapestry of qualities, energies, and expressions that have been associated with the female experience throughout human history.

Yet, to truly understand femininity, we must first shatter the mirror of simplified stereotypes and rigid social constructs that have often confined it.

Femininity isn't about checking boxes or fitting molds—it's about awakening to the divine feminine energy that already resides within you.

Picture this energy as a river, flowing differently through each person it touches. For some, it rushes forth as nurturing rapids of caregiving instincts; for others, it pools into deep waters of creativity, intuition, or emotional intelligence. There is no single "correct" channel for this river to flow, and this understanding forms the bedrock of our exploration.

Throughout history, feminine energy has danced through our stories in a thousand forms. From the Greek goddess Aphrodite, who painted the world in hues of love and beauty, to the Hindu goddess Kali, who wielded transformation like lightning in her hands—each represents a different face of feminine power. These diverse incarnations remind us that femininity encompasses both the gentle morning dew and the fierce storm, both the embracing earth and the transformative flame.

In our modern world, many find themselves struggling to embrace their feminine nature as if trying to catch starlight in cupped hands. Some view femininity as a weakness, while others mistake it for submission or dependency. But true femininity is like the moon itself—a source of immense power that moves oceans, guides rhythms, and illuminates the darkness. It is the force that gives birth not only to human life but to ideas that reshape worlds, art that touches souls, relationships that heal hearts, and communities that change societies.

Chapter Two
The Physical Expression of Femininity

Like a dance between body and spirit, the physical expression of femininity flows far beyond the surface of mere appearance. It's a symphony of movement, energy, and presence that begins in our deepest core and ripples outward into the world. While society often fixates on the outer reflection, true feminine expression is like a flower blooming from within—each petal unfurling in its own perfect time, each movement an authentic expression of the soul within.

Imagine feminine movement as water in motion—fluid, graceful, and ever-changing. Whether in the ancient art of belly dancing, where movements ripple like waves under the moonlight, or in the simple sway of walking down a street, feminine energy favors the circular over the linear, the flowing over the rigid. This natural grace isn't choreographed or forced; it's simply the body's way of speaking its truth. When we allow ourselves to move from this place of natural wisdom, every gesture becomes poetry, every step a verse in the ongoing story of our feminine nature.

Your voice carries another kind of magic—one that can warm hearts like summer sunshine or soothe spirits like a gentle stream. The feminine voice isn't about pitch or performance, but about letting your authentic emotions color your words like watercolors bleeding into paper. It's an instrument that can create spaces of intimacy as comfortable as a warm embrace. When we speak from our feminine essence, our words carry the power to heal, nurture, and transform both ourselves and those around us. The tone, the rhythm, the subtle inflections—all become carriers of deeper meaning and connection.

Physical self-care becomes a sacred ritual when approached through feminine wisdom. Like tending a garden, it's not about forcing growth but nurturing what naturally blooms. This might mean greeting the dawn with gentle yoga stretches, savoring food as if each bite were a blessing, or creating personal ceremonies that honor your body's wisdom. These aren't tasks on an endless to-do list but rather loving conversations with your physical being. Each act of self-care becomes a prayer of gratitude for the vessel that carries our spirit through this world.

Feminine presence transforms spaces like sunlight transforms a room. Rather than commanding attention, it invites connection. Think of how a flower's fragrance naturally draws others closer, or how a warm smile can instantly change the atmosphere of a room. This is feminine energy at work—subtle yet profound, inviting rather than demanding. It's the power to create sanctuary wherever we go, turning ordinary moments into opportunities for beauty and grace. Our presence can soften edges, warm hearts, and create spaces where others feel safe to be their authentic selves.

Even the way we adorn ourselves becomes an art form, a personal expression rather than a compliance with fashion's demands. Choose clothes and accessories like you're selecting colors for a painting—with intention, joy, and a deep understanding of what makes your spirit sing. Each piece we wear can be a celebration of our unique beauty, a way to honor the temple of our body. When we dress from this place of self-love and creative expression, our outer appearance becomes a true reflection of our inner radiance.

Likewise, the physical expression of femininity is also about embracing the cycles and seasons of our bodies. Like the moon waxing and waning, our energy and needs shift in natural rhythms. Learning to honor these cycles—to rest when we need rest, to move when we feel called to move, to speak when our truth rises up—is a part of embodying our feminine wisdom. It's about trusting the deep intelligence of our bodies and allowing ourselves to flow with, rather than against, our natural rhythms.

In every gesture, every word, and every choice we make about how we present ourselves to the world, we have the opportunity to express our feminine essence. This isn't about performing femininity for others, but about allowing our authentic nature to shine through in all its magnificent forms. When we fully embrace our physical expression of femininity, we become living art—each of us a unique and beautiful manifestation of the divine feminine in motion.

Chapter Three
The Emotional and Spiritual Dimensions of Femininity

Imagine your emotional world as a vast ocean—deep, powerful, and full of hidden treasures. The feminine approach to emotions isn't about building walls against these waters but learning to swim with their currents. Like a skilled navigator reading the stars, feminine wisdom teaches us to read our emotional compass, understanding that each feeling carries a message as valuable as an ancient map. Every wave of emotion, whether gentle or stormy, guides us toward deeper self-knowledge and authenticity.

Intuition is your inner lighthouse, sending out beams of guidance through fog and storm. This deep knowledge whispers like wind through leaves, often so subtle you must become still to hear it. Developing intuition is like strengthening a muscle—it requires trust, practice, and the courage to follow its light even when the logical path points elsewhere. Each time you honor this inner voice, it grows stronger, clearer, and more reliable in its gentle urgings toward truth.

Feminine spirituality moves in circles, like the moon waxing and waning, like seasons turning their eternal wheel. By aligning with these natural rhythms—whether they're the moon's phases painted across the sky or the cycles flowing through your own body— you tap into wisdom older than time. These cycles aren't constraints but rather cosmic dances you're invited to join. In this sacred choreography, you learn to honor both the light and shadow aspects of yourself, understanding that both are necessary for wholeness.

Creating sacred space for yourself becomes an art of the heart. Whether it's a corner of your room transformed into an altar or a moment of quiet carved from a busy day, these sanctuaries are like wells of peace you can draw from whenever your spirit thirsts. They're not just physical spaces but doorways to the divine feminine that resides within. Each crystal, candle, or meaningful object placed with intention becomes a bridge between the mundane and the mystical, helping you to anchor your spiritual practice in the physical world.

This journey into feminine spirituality isn't just about personal transformation—it's about remembering. Remembering the ancient ways of being that live in our bones, the wisdom passed down through generations of women, and the power of circles and sisterhood. As you dive deeper into these waters, you'll discover that the greatest mysteries aren't found in distant temples but within your own heart, where the divine feminine has always dwelled, patiently waiting for you to return home to yourself.

Chapter Four
Integrating Femininity in Modern Life

Like a master alchemist, the modern woman must learn to blend the sacred oils of feminine wisdom with the quick-flowing waters of contemporary life. This integration isn't about choosing between two worlds, but rather about creating a unique fusion where ancient wisdom dances with present-day reality.

In the workplace, feminine energy can flow like a hidden stream beneath the surface of traditional structures. Rather than adopting an artificial corporate mask, imagine yourself as a rose growing through concrete—bringing beauty, softness, and natural authority to even the most rigid environments. Your intuitive leadership style might manifest as the ability to nurture team creativity like a master gardener tends to different plants, each requiring its own special care to flourish.

Within relationships, feminine wisdom acts like moonlight casting on the water—illuminating depths that logic alone cannot reach. Whether you're nurturing family bonds, cultivating friendships, or navigating romantic partnerships, your feminine energy creates spaces where authenticity can bloom, and connections can deepen like roots seeking rich soil. This doesn't mean becoming a boundary-less caregiver; rather, think of yourself as a lighthouse—steady in your strength while offering guidance and warmth to others.

Your home becomes a sacred vessel where feminine energy can fully express itself. Like a priestess tending her temple, you create atmospheres that nourish both body and soul. This might mean arranging your space like a carefully composed symphony—each element contributing to a harmonious whole—or establishing rituals that transform everyday moments into opportunities for connection with your feminine essence.

In the digital age, where screens often separate us from our sensual nature, feminine wisdom teaches us to remain anchored in our bodies like trees rooted in ancient earth. This might mean taking "digital sabbaticals," where you trade virtual connections for real-world experiences, or creating mindful transitions between your online and offline worlds, like a butterfly moving gracefully between different gardens.

Self-care in modern life becomes an art of sacred balance. Instead of viewing it as another task on an endless to-do list, approach it as a priestess would approach her daily devotions—with reverence, intention, and a deep understanding of its importance. This might mean crafting morning rituals that align you with your feminine power, like a flower opening to the sun, or creating evening practices that help you flow with natural cycles despite urban schedules.

The greatest challenge—and opportunity—lies in maintaining your connection to feminine wisdom amidst the often masculine-energy-dominated pace of modern life. Think of yourself as a skilled dancer, able to move gracefully between different rhythms while maintaining your own internal beat. Some days, you'll flow like water around obstacles; other days, you'll stand firm like a mountain, unwavering in your truth.

Remember: embracing femininity isn't about reaching for perfection like a distant star, but about letting your inner light shine in its own unique way. As you continue this journey, trust that your feminine wisdom will guide you like an internal compass, leading you toward your own authentic expression of this timeless and transformative energy.

Chapter Five
Sacred Practices - Six Gateways to Feminine Energy

Like a master jeweler selecting precious stones, we've chosen six transformative practices that will help you embody your feminine essence. Each of these gateways offers a unique path to deepening your connection with feminine wisdom, like different paths leading to the same sacred temple.

1. The Morning Ritual - Awakening Your Feminine Flow

Picture yourself as a flower gradually opening to the dawn. Begin each day with a practice we call "The Gentle Awakening":

- Rise 15 minutes before your usual time.
- Light a candle or open your curtains to greet the morning light.
- Move your body in slow, circular motions—stretching like a cat awakening from slumber.
- Write three flowing sentences in your journal, letting your intuition guide your pen.

- Set an intention for carrying your feminine energy through the day, like a perfume you'll wear in your heart.

2. The Sacred Pause - Creating Moments of Presence

In the rush of modern life, this practice is like dropping a pebble into still water. It is recommended three times each day, preferably between tasks or meetings:

- Take three deep breaths, imagining you're breathing in the moonlight.
- Soften your shoulders and jaw, letting tension melt like snow in spring.
- Place one hand over your heart, connecting to your inner wisdom.
- Ask yourself: "What does my feminine spirit need in this moment?"
- Honor whatever answer arises, even if you can only act on it later.

3. The Sensual Feast - Awakening Your Physical Wisdom

Transform an ordinary meal into a ceremony of feminine presence:

- Set your table as if you are preparing an altar with flowers or a beautiful cloth.
- Engage all your senses as you prepare or unwrap your food.
- Eat slowly, savoring each bite like you're tasting starlight.
- Express gratitude for the nourishment, either silently or aloud.
- Notice how this mindful approach affects your digestion and satisfaction.

4. The Circle of Sisters - Cultivating Feminine Connection

Like pearls on a string, we grow stronger when connected. Once a month:

- Gather with 2-4 women you trust (in person or virtually).
- Sit in a circle or create a virtual sacred space.
- Take turns, sharing from your heart while others hold space.
- Offer support without trying to fix or solve.
- End by expressing gratitude for each woman's presence.

5. The Embodied Dance - Moving with Your Feminine Power

This practice is like letting a river flow through your body:

- Choose music that makes your soul sing.

- Close your eyes and begin moving from your womb space.
- Let your movements be circular and flowing, like water.
- Release the need to look "graceful" or choreographed.
- Dance for at least one song, allowing your feminine energy to express itself freely.

6. The Evening Surrender - Honoring Your Cyclical Nature

As the day closes, practice what we call "The Moonlight Release":

- Create a small ritual space in your bedroom.
- Light a candle or use soft lighting.
- Write down what you're releasing from the day.
- Take three items from your space and arrange them beautifully.
- Spend 5 minutes in gentle meditation or prayer.
- End by speaking words of self-love with a focus on your heart chakra and solar plexus.

Remember to approach these practices like you would tend to a garden—with patience, consistency, and loving attention. Some days, your practice will feel as natural as breathing, while others might require more conscious effort. However, both experiences are perfectly valid expressions of your feminine journey.

Start with the practice that calls to you most strongly, like a flower reaching for sunlight. After a week, add another, gradually building your feminine wisdom until these moments of sacred connection become as natural as the moon's phases or the turning of the seasons.

Trust that each small step on this path is transformative, like drops of water slowly filling a well of feminine wisdom. Your practice doesn't need to be perfect—it only needs to be authentic to you, flowing from your heart like a spring from deep earth.

Made in the USA
Middletown, DE
22 March 2025